You Can Estimate, That's Really Great!

Tracy Kompelien

Consulting Editors, Diane Craig, M.A./Reading Specialist
and Susan Kosel, M.A. Education

ABDO
Publishing Company

Published by ABDO Publishing Company, 4940 Viking Drive, Edina, Minnesota 55435.

Copyright © 2007 by Abdo Consulting Group, Inc. International copyrights reserved in all countries. No part of this book may be reproduced in any form without written permission from the publisher. SandCastle™ is a trademark and logo of ABDO Publishing Company.

Printed in the United States.

Credits
Edited by: Pam Price
Curriculum Coordinator: Nancy Tuminelly
Cover and Interior Design and Production: Mighty Media
Photo Credits: Eyewire Images, Photodisc, ShutterStock, Wewerka Photography

Library of Congress Cataloging-in-Publication Data

Kompelien, Tracy, 1975-
    You can estimate, that's really great! / Tracy Kompelien
    p. cm. -- (Math made fun)
    ISBN 10 1-59928-551-7 (hardcover)
    ISBN 10 1-59928-552-5 (paperback)

    ISBN 13 978-1-59928-551-1 (hardcover)
    ISBN 13 978-1-59928-552-8 (paperback)
    1. Estimation theory--Juvenile literature. I. Title. II. Series.

QA276.8.K666 2007
519.5'44--dc22

                                                          2006015299

SandCastle Level: Transitional

SandCastle™ books are created by a professional team of educators, reading specialists, and content developers around five essential components—phonemic awareness, phonics, vocabulary, text comprehension, and fluency—to assist young readers as they develop reading skills and strategies and increase their general knowledge. All books are written, reviewed, and leveled for guided reading, early reading intervention, and Accelerated Reader® programs for use in shared, guided, and independent reading and writing activities to support a balanced approach to literacy instruction. The SandCastle™ series has four levels that correspond to early literacy development. The levels help teachers and parents select appropriate books for young readers.

Emerging Readers
(no flags)

Beginning Readers
(1 flag)

Transitional Readers
(2 flags)

Fluent Readers
(3 flags)

These levels are meant only as a guide. All levels are subject to change.

To estimate

means to make a guess that is close to the exact amount or size of something. It does not matter if you get the right answer. You just try to get as close as you can.

Words used to estimate:
about
bigger than
guess
in between
less than
more than
round
smaller than

A  is smaller than a .

An

is bigger than

a .

A is more than a .

A

is less than

a .

Here are between

5 and 10 .

Here are about

15  .

You Can Estimate, That's Really Great!

**Darlene has about
30 jelly beans.**

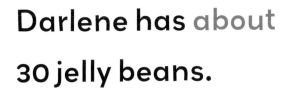

You can estimate
the amount
by rounding to
the nearest 5 or 10.

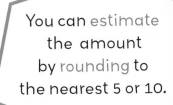

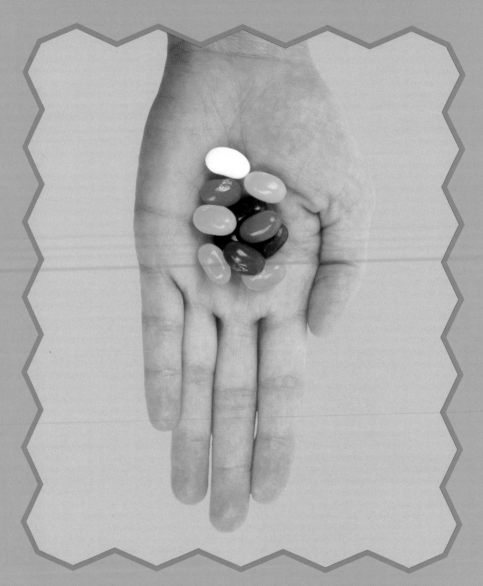

twelve
12

Her friend Eugene has fewer than 15.

> I know what 15 looks like, and this looks like there is a smaller amount than 15.

fourteen
14

Darlene puts her beans together with Eugene's. They have about 45, and that's no jive!

I have about 30 jelly beans. We round the number of Eugene's to 15. When we add 15 to 30, we can estimate that we have about 45 jelly beans.

Estimating Every Day!

I like to guess how many bites it will take to eat my cereal.

I make a guess before I start eating. Then I check my estimate by counting how many spoonfuls I eat!

eighteen

18

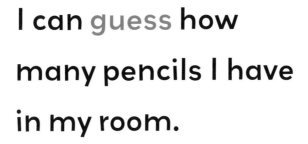

I can guess how many pencils I have in my room.

Look at my pencils and make a good guess about how many there are. Then count them and see if your estimate is close!

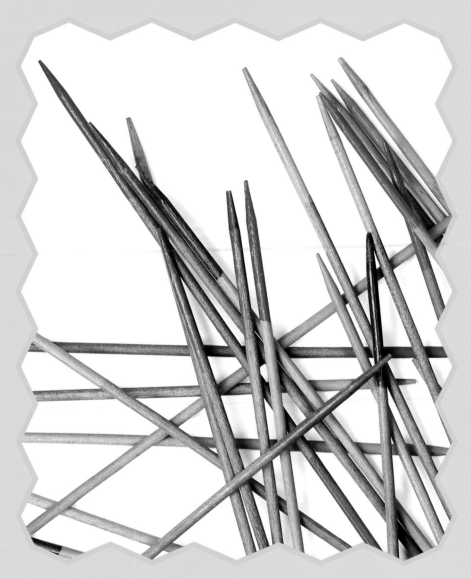

twenty
20

To estimate how many sticks I have, I round to the nearest 10.

To round, I take a good guess, then I round the guess to the nearest 10.

Can you estimate how many steps it is from your school desk to the chalkboard?

Imagine how many steps it would take to walk from your desk to the chalkboard. Walk and count the steps you take to check your estimate!

Glossary

greater than – a value that is higher than another.

guess – to give an answer based on what you think might be true.

less than – a value that is smaller than another.

round – to change a number to another number that is close in value, such as the nearest 5 or 10.